EFFECTIVE SUPERVISION

IN THE OFFICE

EFFECTIVE SUPERVISION IN THE OFFICE

by Mel White

Revised by Paul Southon

The Industrial Society

First published 1964 by
The Industrial Society
Peter Runge House
3 Carlton House Terrace
London SW1Y 5DG
Telephone: 01–839 4300

Third edition, 1989
© *The Industrial Society, 1964, 1970, 1989*

ISBN 0 85290 428 2

British Library Cataloguing in Publication Data:
White, Mel
   Effective supervision in the office. — 3rd ed.
   1. Management. Supervision
   I Title II.   Southon, Paul III.   Industrial Society
   IV.   Series
   658. 3'02

Typeset by Senator Graphics, London
Printed and bound in Great Britain by Belmont Press, Northampton

CONTENTS

FOREWORD

Whatever the discipline or level of management, the responsibilities of managers are many and various. It is their job to produce results with essentially just two resources — people and time.

To maximise the potential of both, most managers need some reminders and basic guidelines to help them.

The Notes for Managers series provides succinct yet comprehensive coverage of key management issues and skills. The short time it takes to read each title will pay dividends in terms of utilising one of those key resources — people.

This book describes the people management responsibilities of the office supervisor, controller, or those immediately responsible for the work of a section. It is concerned with the practical actions that the work group leader needs to take in order to achieve results through those in the group.

As the office supervisor is a vital link in the management chain, this book will help supervisors improve and develop the skills that they require in order to be an effective member of the management team.

ALISTAIR GRAHAM
Director, The Industrial Society

1

WHAT IS A SUPERVISOR?

Before talking about supervision, we must be clear about who we are directing our advice to: what is a supervisor?

Strictly speaking, a supervisor is anyone in charge of others — the *Oxford Dictionary* suggests an administrative or advisory official. The definition could include, in its broadest sense, the directors of most organisations, and is indeed true, for it covers anyone in charge of others who has objectives to meet.

Not unnaturally, many of the items discussed in this book will apply equally to all levels of management and, no doubt, we have all had experiences where our more senior managers should have applied themselves to some of the basic principles contained herein! But take care . . . remember that well known saying: 'All sins start one level above mine, and isn't it strange that they seem to get promoted at the same rate as I do!' Get your own house in order first. When you manage well, you will quite naturally influence those around you.

However, the level that we are specifically aiming at here is the first line of management: undoubtedly the most difficult position of them all; the buffer between the policy making higher levels and the work force that transform those policies into ACTION. Thus, one of the basic essentials that we need at this level is the ability to make things happen; to promote ACTION.

In our offices around the country, this level is known by many names, from supervisor, through section head/head of section, to junior manager, and even director in companies that believe small is beautiful and who organise themselves into small sections.

That is just semantics. What is important is that they are the leaders of the work group, the interface between the work force and management, the people who get things done through the efforts of their work group. What does the leader require to do this? What abilities do you need?

The supervisor's needs

You must: be in charge of a work group of less than 15 people so that you can treat the members of the group as individuals and delegate to them effectively; enjoy the trust and confidence of the staff, and can begin to do so if you are able to tell them in advance about policies or changes that will affect them; participate while enjoying good working relations; take risks where necessary, yet be patient; ensure that your group is well organised and trained to do the job; set up excellent communications with your staff, your colleagues and your boss. Most of all, you must accept the responsibilities of leadership.

Discipline

One of a supervisor's chief responsibilities is for discipline. But what is discipline? There is a school of thought which says that properly handled staff should not need to be disciplined, but isn't this being a little unrealistic? Whenever people work together there must be certain rules and some personal freedom must be sacrificed in order to get the job done; if we did not have order we would not have efficiency.

Discipline is often thought of in terms of fear and punishment, on the assumption that only fear will persuade people to keep to the rules. But punishment represents the *failure* of discipline, and if we expect the worst from our staff we are likely to get it. Conversely, if we treat staff fairly and with understanding we can expect respect, loyalty, and compliance in return.

Discipline must not mean domination. Staff will accept rules and conditions if they can see the reasons for them and if they are just. Positive control is a system of accepted behaviour, not an imposed behaviour, and is an area requiring concentrated effort by the supervisor (*see Effective Discipline*, in this series).

What the supervisor needs to know

Later, we shall look at the 'tools of management' in greater detail, but let us now look at the supervisor in terms of what needs to be understood to be effective.

Job knowledge

Clearly, you must have a thorough knowledge of the work which is processed by your team but, equally important, you must have a thorough knowledge of your responsibilities. Your section and the people who work for you are not an isolated unit; they form part of a larger team — the organisation as a whole — and the supervisor needs to have a good knowledge of the company, its aims and its standards.

Do you know the answers to the questions in Appendix 1? The answers to these and similar questions will provide some idea of the framework within which you work.

You are bound by the policies of your company, so, if you are to be effective you need to be familiar with them.

Accountability

Do you know your place and your team's place in the organisation? You have probably seen your company's organisation chart which, however helpful, tends to over-simplify. Things are never quite so straightforward, as your answers to the questions in Appendix 2 will show. Make sure you know the answers; it is important for you, and your staff, that you have a clear idea of where you belong in the organisation. Too many supervisors are kept in the dark on such matters. Many more have even less idea about what precisely their job entails.

Job description

Like anyone else, you cannot work effectively unless you know what your jobs is. In some organisations, you may be given a written detailed job description, in others only a general directive. Either way, the important thing is that you need to be clear in your own mind about the responsibilities and the extent of your authority. Furthermore, your effectiveness is increased if your superior is clear about your responsibilities and authority as supervisor.

It is impossible to set down a comprehensive list of factors which, in many offices, are the responsibilities of the supervisors. However, some of these factors are shown in Appendix 3. There will be others which apply in your company and can be added to the list.

If you haven't got a written job description, set down in writing what you think your key areas of responsibility are, and then ask your boss to set down what he or she thinks your job is. The results could be illuminating, and rewarding.

2

LEADING AND MOTIVATING

Even in the most materialistic of today's modern industries, the wage bill is likely to be the largest single expenditure. Therefore, to remain competitive, companies require to get 'the best out of their people' and this responsibility falls largely to the first line manager level.

Leadership

Having considered the knowledge supervisors require, we can now explore how they can test their knowledge by applying the various 'tools of management' which were mentioned earlier. According to our definition, the job of supervisor is to get things done through people. As the person responsible and accountable for the activities of staff, a supervisor's aim must be to make full use of their strengths, skills, inventiveness and any other abilities they may have, so that every person is giving of their best at work. The effective supervisor must be capable of getting the utmost from his or her staff and needs, therefore, to develop the ability to lead others.

Basically, the effectiveness of supervisors as leaders depends on their ability to influence, and be influenced by, the groups in their charge and the individuals who make up those groups in the carrying out of a common task. This can be illustrated diagrammatically as below:

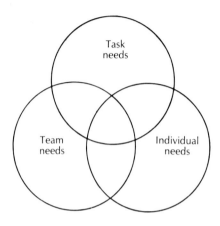

Supervisors must ensure that the required tasks or jobs are completed satisfactorily while, at the same time, supervising their groups in such a way that the group work and group identity are maintained and developed. At the same time, they must recognise that each person who makes up the team is an individual with needs, hopes, ideas and so on which must be met if the individual is to be effective. If a supervisor pays too much attention to achieve the task at whatever cost, sooner or later the team will begin to disintegrate. Similarly, by ignoring individual needs, a supervisor fails to spot the rotten apple, and very soon there may be a rotten barrel, and consequently the performance of the team will suffer and the team may indeed disintegrate.

The model above indicates that the effective leader must work at all three areas if a high level of performance is to be sustained.

There are certain steps the supervisor can take to help achieve the task while maintaining the needs of the group and individuals. However, you may care to supplement these steps by analysing your own performance in the three areas and drawing up a checklist of points to be considered in the leadership situation.

Achieving the task

A supervisor must:

1 have a clear idea about what the task is
2 understand how the task fits into the objectives of the company
3 plan how the task will be accomplished, in consultation with others, including the team
4 define and provide the resources needed, i.e. time, authority, staff, equipment, and so on
5 ensure that the organisational structure allows the task to be achieved effectively
6 brief the team so that they are totally clear as to the objective
7 monitor the action and control progress
8 evaluate the results, learning from success as well as failure.

Building and maintaining a team

A company or firm is a complex organisation. Because it is complex, it requires co-ordinated action if it is to be efficient. We talk of 'everyone pulling in the same direction'. The difference between a collection of individuals and a cohesive group or team is that, in a team, the individuals have a willingness and ability to work together — to co-operate. They can do this when they are made aware of their common purpose. Individuals in work groups often have different and separate tasks, not common tasks. But these individual tasks invariably have a common purpose. It is the leader's job to make them aware of what it is. This is how co-operation is won.

Each team has its own personality, its own power, its own attitudes, its own standards and its own needs. A successful leader understands this and studies the group *as* a group.

Here is a short checklist to help a supervisor build and maintain his or her team.

1 Get them together regularly in order to:
   ● brief them about objectives and their achievement. 'What we are trying to achieve and how we are doing'

- consult them for their ideas, opinions, suggestions for improvement.
2 Talk about 'we', instead of 'I'.
3 Help to resolve conflicts when they occur.
4 Speak up for the team when this is necessary.
5 Organise them to make the widest use of their talents.
6 Establish common standards and stick to them.

It follows that, if you actively involve your team in determining objectives — in choosing working methods, in reorganising work schedules, in solving problems, in making decisions — you will have the team behind you and will be better able to change team practices than if you give separate instructions to each individual member or impose new orders and instructions. By involving the team, you will be more effective in bringing about needed change and better implementation of the new procedures.

Meeting individual needs

This requires each supervisor to have some knowledge about what makes people 'tick', particularly what makes them tick at work, so that they can be motivated to give better and more productive work.

Traditionally, of course, work has been regarded as an unpleasant necessity rather than a potential motivator. For this reason, many older supervisors and managers still consider it necessary to entice people to work by promises of rewards and so on, or make them work by threats, or both.

Fortunately, this attitude is changing (though not as rapidly as one might think or hope) thanks to forward-thinking management who, influenced to a large degree by such behavioural scientists as McGregor, Maslow, and Herzberg, are now realising that people want to work, like responsibility and need to achieve. The challenge for the supervisor is to provide opportunities for individuals to satisfy these needs.

People work for many reasons: to attain high levels of material comfort; for recognition and prestige; for social service; and for the work itself, if it is sufficiently interesting and challenging. There are probably many other reasons, but the real problem is in trying to decide why people do *not* work as hard as they could. There have been many surveys on this question, and broadly speaking the results can be categorised under these headings:

- bad working conditions
- fear of redundancy, changes, inadequacy, etc.
- boredom
- personal worries
- poor supervision
- feeling of unimportance
- lack of incentive
- poor relationships with colleagues
- lack of information about the job and surroundings.

You can probably add to the following list of suggestions for positive action the supervisor can take to lift people from minimal performance to efficient, effective producers.

1 Help staff to realise that work can be a satisfying, integral part of life itself.
2 Provide clear targets by which their performance can be measured.
3 Consider any incentives, financial and otherwise.
4 Give praise where praise is due, and be specific.
5 Keep people informed of any changes, so that they have a sense of security.
6 Respect your staff as individuals.
7 Involve staff in the overall job so that their interest is developed.
8 Keep a close eye on working conditions. Notice defects and put forward recommendations for improvements.
9 Be constantly on the lookout for improved layouts and methods.

To provide the right atmosphere and opportunities for each individual to achieve satisfaction and self-fulfilment is probably the most difficult of the three areas of the supervisor's job but, if successful, it can also be the most rewarding.

3

TRAINING FOR
EFFICIENCY

If all jobs are to provide interest and challenge, it follows that they will be continually progressing and changing. In turn, this means that the job holder often will require training to attain the level of competence required for the larger job. Let us now look, therefore, at the supervisor's responsibilities for training; training not just of new staff in specific skills, but of existing staff whose jobs are to be expanded or who are to become more efficient and productive.

If we define training as the process of acquiring skills and knowledge to respond effectively to certain situations, it follows that, if there is a gap between the standard of performance required by the supervisor and the performance actually achieved by the subordinate, it is the supervisor's responsibility to take action to fill that gap by training. This is one aspect of training. There are others which we shall discuss later on.

Because supervisors are accountable for the job performance of their staff, they must be aware of their responsibilities and of the essential functions of training. They also need to know the methods to make the training more effective.

Responsibilities

A supervisor has a two-fold responsibility for training:

1   to develop deputies and to train immediate subordinates, encouraging them in their turn to train theirs
2   to ensure that a comprehensive system of training is established and maintained in the unit, seeing that everyone has the opportunity to develop to their full potential.

If these responsibilities are accepted and followed, they point the way to greater efficiency and effectiveness over a number of areas such as:

- the development of staff
- high quality and economical production
- efficient and smooth organisation
- individual effectiveness of staff
- greater flexibility.

They also help maintain team and individual needs by giving staff a sense of responsibility, by creating good relationships, by developing co-operation and by creating an identification with the interests and objectives of the organisation as a whole.

Realising responsibilities and doing something about them are usually two different things; how then does the supervisor perform the training role? The training function itself is a four-fold operation.

1 Assessing the needs for training

Draw up a plan showing who needs training and for what. As supervisor you, more than anyone in the organisation, are aware of:

- the standard of personnel necessary to perform the job
- the nature of the work being done and the skill required to perform the job
- the gaps in skill and performance standards required.

2 Organising training

Even though your organisation may have a training programme, the supervisor is the essential link between the training officer and the office and, more often than not, any on-the-job training is performed by supervisors or a member of their staff.

If you are doing the training, you need to be thoroughly prepared by knowing and using job specifications and breakdowns. Training manuals should be used whenever possible.

3 Carrying out training

There are many methods of training, ranging from on-the-job coaching to university or college courses. Similarly, there are many training techniques, all of which have their pros and cons: lectures, discussion groups, role playing, video, audio and computer based packages, etc.

Most of us, however, are concerned primarily with training 'at the desk' by demonstration and delegation techniques (see Chapter 4).

4 Evaluating training

Here, the supervisor must take steps to check the effectiveness of the training, i.e. how well the results of training meet the original need. It is also an opportunity to amend the training programme in the light of its effectiveness and, of course, to maintain training records.

How effective are you?

There are many spheres of work where the supervisor needs to think about the training element, and the above four points should be applied when thinking about such work aspects as:

- the introduction of new staff to the company
- the introduction of new staff to the department; its function, customs, hours, amenities, team, etc.
- systematic training of new staff in a specific job
- improving performance by retraining on existing job
- developing staff for promotion
- developing staff for greater efficiency.

Try to assess your own effectiveness in the training areas by setting down a checklist of points to consider when arranging the training of your staff. Have you got a plan for each of the areas mentioned above? There are probably other training areas you can add.

Many aspects of supervisors' effectiveness can be seen in the way they train their staff, as the following questions demonstrate.

- How well do things work out when the supervisor is not there?
- To what extent has the supervisor made provision for things to work out well?
- How has the performance of a supervisor's staff improved since they joined his/her section or took on additional responsibilities?
- When special demands are put upon the section how well do the staff cope?

Remember that the trainee of today is the supervisor of tomorrow and, if for no other reason, the supervisor must be involved in the training.

'Regardless of how much training is done in a company before an employee reports to a particular supervisor, the supervisor must still do some training. Actually, giving work assignments, inspecting work assignments, inspecting work and upgrading performance, should still be thought of as training.'

Norman Maier, *Psychology of Industry.*

4

DEVELOPING STAFF — DELEGATION

Most supervisors practise delegation, or think they do. Do you delegate? What is delegation? A few sample answers to the latter might be:

> 'Sharing out the work.'
> 'Getting someone to do a specific job.'
> 'Passing on the routine jobs so that I've got more time.'
> 'Organising the work so that everyone is occupied.'

What is really being defined is 'allocation'. Delegation is *more* than allocation.

Delegation can be defined as giving to others part of *your* job which is *your* responsibility contained in *your* job descripton/ specification — giving you more time to manage (what you are paid for!) and your staff more responsibility and fulfilment.

Delegation is the key to successful management. After all, could the Prime Minister or the Chairman of ICI be effective in their jobs if they were not able to delegate?

You will become more effective if you learn the art — but it is not to be taken lightly for it is a risky business. Remember that you can delegate RESPONSIBILITY and the AUTHORITY to complete a job, but you cannot delegate the ACCOUNTABILITY. In other words, although you make someone else responsible for a part of your job, you still carry the can at the end of the day.

So why delegate?

● Effective delegation frees supervisors to think, plan ahead, and gives them time to do the *supervisory* part of their job.

14

- It develops the skills and potential of the subordinates and is an essential part of the training process.
- It allows full use to be made of the staff's specialist skills.
- Staff feel more involved with the job if they are given responsibility. They derive more satisfaction from their work.

Having considered a few of the reasons why we should delegate, it is useful to look at the reasons why it goes wrong:

- it involves people
- lack of planning and training
- fear of the ability of a junior
- we think we can do the job better ourselves
- many supervisors are loath to relinquish detail — they enjoy certain technical features of the job from which they were promoted and want to carry on doing them
- because of the risk involved — mistakes may occur
- failure to make it stick — the subordinate wants you to make the decisions so, in the end, you take the job back
- indistinct definition of what it is you are actually delegating — the subordinate does not really know what is expected, so nothing is done
- having delegated the job, you fail to let go of the strings and let subordinates do it their way
- it takes time in the short-term.

Effective delegation

First you must decide what jobs you are able to delegate and here you must be harsh with yourself — too many supervisors think that *all* of their work is important. Start by asking yourself: *'What jobs am I doing at present?'* Make a list of *all* the jobs you have to do over a period. Alongside each job write down the answer to: *'Why do I do this job?'* Because you always do it, because you like doing it; because your boss or legislation requires you to do it. These could be some of the answers, there will be others.

Next, ask yourself: *'Must I do it, and why?'* A 'yes' answer many have an unsatisfactory reason which, if investigated may turn the 'yes' into 'no'. Assuming that there are some 'no' answers, you must then ask yourself: *'To whom should I delegate the job?'* It may be, of course, that there is no-one in your staff at present who can do the job — you must therefore ask yourself the final question: *'Who should I be training?'*

The process of delegation

The actual process of delegation is very much akin to effective training and the principles are the same. Consider, if you will, a particular job which you feel can be delegated to a member of your staff. Having created a desire in your subordinate to take on a new, responsible job, by explaining why you want the job done and how it will help career development, you proceed to hand over the job in five easy stages.

Stage 1

While the subordinate is sitting alongside you, demonstrate how the job is done by doing it yourself. The trainee is asked to watch and criticise. It is most important that, even at this early stage, subordinates should be asked to criticise — a 'new look' at the job can often find ways to improve the method, for you may be behind the times yourself. In any event, get the fresh approach from the outset.

Stage 2

Having demonstrated the job, the next stage is to get the subordinate to do it. You should brief the subordinate, allow for questions, and then let the trainee do the job while you watch and comment when necessary.

Stage 3

The subordinate now does the job at his/her own desk without supervision. Beforehand, however, you will check the person's knowledge by again briefing and asking questions. While the trainee is doing the job you should be available to answer questions and, at the end, the subordinate will report whether or not he/she has succeeded.

Stage 4

You have now reached the stage where you can give the subordinate the job to do without asking questions. At the end the subordinate should report back to you.

Stage 5

You will now arrange for the subordinate to receive the job straight from source, i.e. where you used to get it from. This is a way of ensuring that you have handed over the responsibility and authority of the job. Obviously, as supervisor and, therefore, ultimately responsible for all the work in the office, you must reserve the right to check the job from time to time.

You may have noticed that at any stage up to the last you could have discontinued the delegation process if things were not going well. Indeed, you would not proceed to Stage 5 unless you were satisfied that the subordinate could do the job and take on the responsibility and authority. How much better it is to plan the handing over in this way rather than 'give' someone a job to do and still be doubtful as to whether or not the person will do it correctly. This five-stage process is an effective guarantee against the occurrence of many of the points of error and confusion referred to earlier.

One last word on this important subject: we have already said that delegation as a supervisory 'tool' is essential, but it must be made to work. You need to recognise the ability of your staff, you must have complete trust in them, you must have a genuine desire to develop them and finally, you must delegate systematically (see *Delegation,* in this series).

5

DEVELOPING STAFF — APPRAISAL

We have already discussed the importance of setting clear targets to improve efficiency, and monitoring performance on a day-to-day basis. However, it is also important to discuss performance with your staff over a longer period: six months or a year.

Lots of companies do this for their new staff, but once the 'probationary period' is past, the procedure stops — as if experienced staff do not need to know how they are doing!

The Industrial Society advocates that *all* staff need to know the following.

- Who is my boss? — if there is any doubt in this area, approach management for clarification.
- What is my job? Job description/specification.
- How am I doing?
- What is expected of me?
- How do I get there and what help is there available?

Appraisal interviews

Set aside a couple of hours for each of your staff at least once a year. Tell them in advance that you want to discuss their work and get them to think about some areas like:

- re-read job description — is it still relevant
- problems in the job
- ideas to solve
- any specific help required.

Think of this appraisal interview as 'a conversation with a purpose' rather than you giving a verdict on their competence. Make use of the interview checklist in Chapter 6: it will help you prepare.

If your company has an appraisal scheme, fill in the form as a result of your discussion, making sure that, on completion of the interview, both parties are quite clear on what has been decided and in what timescale. Then monitor to ensure ACTION.

6

PEOPLE PROBLEMS — INTERVIEWING

Supervisors often complain that they would do their job much better if they did not have so many 'people problems' to deal with. How often do you complain that you have spent the greater part of your day 'listening to so-and-so's problems' or 'getting involved in personal problems' or 'telling staff off for mistakes' and, as a result, you 'haven't been able to do a stroke of work'.

The fact is, people are your work, or ought to be, and you should be pleased that your staff have sufficient confidence in you to want to discuss their personal problems with you or air their grievances directly, rather than through your boss. Supervisors who do not get involved in these matters are being horribly misled if they think that problems do not exist in their sections and they should take a long, hard look at how they handle their staff.

Problem-solving

Those of us who do meet staff problems are often in the face-to-face situation of an interview, without really appreciating what it is we are trying to do. Interviews, to most of us, are something the personnel department do when they are seeking new staff and yet, quite simply, an interview normally involves two people who meet together to discuss a particular problem in order to solve it. Supervisors, generally, are involved very largely with the 'personal problem'; the disciplinary and the grievance interview. There are other, more formal, interviews like selection and appraisal which we may perform from time to time, but the bulk of a supervisor's interviewing is concerned with the question: 'Can I help you?' in the day-to-day situation (see *Interviewing Skills*, Communications Skills Guide, The Industrial Society).

The discipline interview

To most of us, a discipline interview is a 'one-off' job — giving a member of staff a rocket for an offence and, probably, promptly forgetting it and certainly not holding it against the person. The snag is, too often the offence occurs again. If you looked closely at the discipline interviews you have held recently, the chances are that most of them will concern the same individuals time and time again, for the same old offence. Your 'rocket' has a temporary effect, but soon they will slide into the old routine and the process will start all over again.

There are many reasons for this, of course. Psychology plays a great part; basically, the characters who are always offending are those who enjoy the notoriety the offences create, who enjoy being the centre of attention. Sooner or later, their colleagues will realise that they are carrying them, and will exert their own discipline. If, however, 'later' is too long, it is important that you show firmness. If your reprimands continue to fail then you and that person must part company, for everyone's sake.

Failing to achieve standards

It is important at this stage to draw the distinction between the habitual offender and the odd member of staff who, from time to time, cannot achieve the required standards. In this case, you have a duty to consider your discipline as far more than a one-off rocket. Your objective must be not only to correct the mistake, but to take positive steps to ensure that it doesn't occur again. Often this will involve additional training and guidance or, if it is a 'rules' offence, you must spend time searching for the root cause of the trouble. A deliberate flouting of the rules is rare, so you owe it to your staff to dig deep and then encourage the offender to settle down and improve.

Legislation

The way we discipline people at work is now affected by employment law. Much of the recent employment legislation seeks to protect the employee from unfair treatment by the employer. The Industrial Relations Code of Practice, introduced in 1972, and the later ACAS Code *Disciplinary practice and procedures in employment* give practical guidance to employers on various aspects of discipline and dismissal among other things (*see also Guide to employment practices*, in this series).

As a result of legislation, your company or firm will have updated its disciplinary and grievance procedures. It is essential that you have a good working knowledge of your own company procedures and are quite sure that you know how to apply them and when they apply.

The personal problem interview

It was suggested earlier that it is a tribute to you if your staff are willing to discuss their personal problems with you. You should do everything you can to promote this desire, which is so vital to good staff relationships. However, personal problem interviews are extremely difficult and, if badly handled, can do untold harm. This is not to say that they should be left to the 'experts' in the personnel department; on the contrary, you should be willing and capable of handling them, up to a point. Your role is that of a listener: the outlet for the problem; the sympathetic ear to provide someone with an opportunity to talk. By talking about their problems, they can often be reduced and, indeed, a solution may appear simply by talking through the problem.

The pitfall comes when you are asked for advice and help. You must be extremely careful about this. Advice, even after careful deliberation and firm conviction that it is the right advice, could be wrong, or bad, or unworkable, or all three. However kind-hearted and well-meaning you are trying to be, there is nothing more calculated to breed resentment in staff than to be given inadequate advice or help when they have a personal problem.

Your job should be limited to providing factual information which you possess in your capacity as a supervisor, acting as a 'forwarding agent' by passing on the problem to the appropriate experts, being sympathetic, and offering encouragement to the employee to work it out independently.

The grievance interview

When staff have a grumble or grievance, they cannot be working effectively and, they will probably not be satisfied by simply being given an opportunity to talk about it. They will want positive action and, in both your interests, you have got to provide it.

The great difficulty, of course, is that most of the complaints your staff have will have been heard many times before from others, and there is a great tendency for supervisors to 'play down' the complaint. Do not fall into the trap: if an employee complains then, to that person, it is important and you must treat the complaint with respect and understanding. Listen to the complaint, let the employee know that you are trying to help, but do not succumb to the temptation of making promises to cool things down — otherwise that person and others will very soon latch on to the knowledge that all their complaints are going to be settled to *their* entire satisfaction.

Check the grievance, investigate the complaint, get the facts and, above all, do not be rushed into making a decision which, chances are, you will regret.

Do not ignore the petty things which often go wrong and which people are always complaining about. Draughts, poor lighting, inefficient equipment and such like, can create big problems if allowed to go unheeded. You must provide the right physical working environment because, although these things may not 'start' trouble, they help to inflate other problems.

Pre-emptive action

Staff who are well selected and well trained are far less likely to cause trouble. People doing jobs beyond their ability will be disgruntled; people doing something below their ability will be frustrated. If these situations are occurring, liaise with your personnel department so that they have a better knowledge of your requirements.

Learn to anticipate trouble — use your nose! The supervisor who anticipates the small troubles and disputes, and builds up a good team spirit, is not likely to be much worried by discipline problems.

Be as ready to give praise for good work as you are to criticise when things go wrong. Do not let your staff say: 'The only time I'm noticed in this place is when things go wrong'. People like to feel that good work is noticed, and it encourages greater effort.

Have a system which enables you to discuss formally with your staff their strengths and their weaknesses, so that they know how they are getting on. Do this regularly, every six months say, so that staff will know that they have every opportunity to air their complaints and personal grievances. Finally, stick to your company procedure!

Checklist for interviewing

Although every interview is unique, experience has shown that good interviewers have some procedures in common.

Method

Have a simple, flexible plan to work from. This should cover the three main areas of any interview which are as follows.

Preparation:
- clarify the objective of the interview
- get all available facts
- decide on the questions you want to ask.

Interview itself:
- allow enough time and, so far as is practicable, try to ensure privacy
- put the interviewee at ease by being approachable and courteous
- explain yourself clearly
- stimulate response by asking open questions and by avoiding the 'yes/no' answers
- let the interviewee do most of the talking
- use your eyes: watch for personality clues
- LISTEN.

Mechanics:
- decide on a plan of order
- take notes but tell the interviewee why you are taking them
- judge on the facts

- don't be afraid to use 'pauses' — the inexperienced interviewer tends to feel embarrassed and fills the pauses with unnecessary verbiage
- finish cleanly — avoid the tendency to ramble on, and summarise concisely so that both parties are in no doubt as to what has been decided.

Follow-up
- check the facts where necessary
- check, and be seen to check, subsequent events, i.e. monitor.

Experience

It may be depressing but, more often than not, the good interviewer is the experienced interviewer.

Self-knowledge

Recognise your own prejudices, attitudes and qualities before you try to take a reading of somebody else.

Emotional stability

Don't get emotionally involved in the interviews. You must give a balanced, fair judgement, based on facts, and you are hardly likely to do this if you get 'involved'.

Listening ability

A very difficult habit to cultivate, but essential if you want to do your job effectively. Remember, if it is a monologue it cannot be a dialogue; if you explain your ideas you won't learn those of the person you are interviewing; and if you don't listen you cannot help nor communicate.

7

KEEPING STAFF
INFORMED

The increasing expectations of people demand a new approach to our disciplinary code. 'Do it or else . . .' no longer works. A more constructive, positive approach is necessary, aimed at preventing problems rather than punishing offenders.

Probably the most essential function of any supervisor's job is the need to communicate to staff. But, frequently, this is an aspect of work which many supervisors perform least effectively.

What to communicate

Where then, do supervisors go wrong? Essentially, the fault probably lies in what we really mean by communication. We believe we are communicating if we take steps to pass on to staff instructions, or orders, or information which normally requires certain action from the staff. Invariably when that 'action' is incorrect or inadequate we are inclined to blame staff rather than look to ourselves. We need not look too far for the reason — if we took the trouble to *ensure* that what we were communicating was *understood*, we would be far more effective.

It can fairly be said that you will get the best from your staff if they understand not only what they have to do but also WHY they have to do it and how it contributes to the success of the organisation. Furthermore, the supervisor should endeavour to gain *acceptance* from staff. It is recognised that if the supervisor is to get action or reaction to any instruction, order, or information, the staff will be more wholly committed if they can accept the communication. This is not to be confused with agreement. If, however, dissension and disagreement cannot be expressed and discussed with the supervisor, there can be little hope of the staff being committed (or accepting) the communication. Therefore, the reasons *why* (not just the *how* and the *what*) of the decision, instruction, or information, must be communicated. Keeping staff fully informed is a continuous process and is a vital part of a supervisor's job.

There are a number ways of communicating available, but supervisors tend to rely on three: notices and memos, casual methods and face-to-face meetings.

Writing memos

Notices and memos are fine for factual information, but you cannot guarantee that your staff even read the notice, let alone understand it. If what you are communicating requires positive understanding, you will not ensure it by using notices and memos; you must use another method supported, perhaps, by a written confirmation of your message.

Being available

Many supervisors like to assure their staff that they have an 'ever-open door' or, better, because they are always walking around the office, they can be stopped at any time if someone has a query or wants a few words of advice. This is an excellent arrangement and, if you have a reputation for 'being available', cling to it. However, don't assume that this casual method is sufficient; it isn't. When the pressure is on, you close your office door and omit walking round the office — you don't communicate.

Regular team briefing

Essentially, the best method of communicating is on a face-to-face basis with your team. In this way you not only ensure understanding but, by being with them, you can get feedback from the staff; you can tell how they feel about the message or the change, or whatever.

Don't be one of those supervisors bad at communication because:

- they claim to be too busy
- they retain information that should be passed on because it gives them a feeling of superiority
- they pass on only what has to be done and not why, with the attitude that staff are just there to carry out instructions
- they do not, when they tell one, tell all concerned; they do not really accept that communication is part of their job anyway.

Barriers

If we think of communication as a two-way exchange between people, i.e. the sender issuing the message and the receiver signalling that the message is understood, we must now go on to discuss the barriers which are present between the sender and receiver; barriers which must be overcome if we are to be effective. Here are some of them — you can probably think of many more:

- differences in the personality and attitudes of individuals
- differences in the personality and attitudes of groups
- people's fears, prejudices and emotions
- lack of ability by those communicating
- deliberate blockage of information
- verbal distortion due to accent, slang or language differences
- technical jargon which can only be understood by the expert
- the grapevine found in all offices, but which almost always denigrates the reasons why the decision, instruction, change of procedure, appointment, etc, was made or taken.

Effective communication

To communicate effectively you must be systematic — you must have things so arranged that your staff know that, whenever anything occurs which is likely to affect them, they will have an opportunity to discuss it with you in a structured feedback situation. In this way, while you will never altogether dispose of the grapevine, you will minimise its effectiveness and, moreover, you will ensure that your staff will understand what you are communicating.

If you approach the whole business of keeping your staff in the picture in this way, you cannot fail to arouse their enthusiasm. If you fail, your staff will either be indifferent to you or, worse, actively resentful. Remember the following points.

- Be accessible: do not hide away in your own office.
- Keep your staff informed of any change in the organisation, or methods of work, or introduction of new machinery, or any matter that is likely to affect them. Give them the opportunity to express their opinion and to participate in any decision affecting their work.
- Never ignore any grievance or unrest. Make sure that your staff come to you with any problem or grievance.
- Learn to give directions clearly and to be understood by your staff.
- Keep your boss fully informed of your staff's needs, views, and reactions to any impending change, as well as of the state of the work.
- Discuss with your staff any outstanding good work or any shortcomings, and keep your boss informed on both counts.
- Encourage new ideas, suggestions and criticisms.
- Hold regular meetings with your staff to keep them informed (see Team briefing, in this series).

One last word about these regular meetings; it can be said by some supervisors that they see their staff often enough and they would have nothing to talk about if they met with them on a formal basis. It can more accurately be suggested that supervisors who cannot organise regular meetings with their staff to discuss progress, changes, training, organisation and many other important subjects, are most inadequate supervisors. Appendix 4 gives additional examples of subjects to cover in team briefing.

8

KEEPING STAFF SAFE

Remember that under the Health and Safety at Work Act 1974, it is EVERYBODY'S responsibility to ensure that the work place is safe and fit to be worked in, and, in your capacity as the first line of management, you have a legal responsibility to ensure that your workforce is kept safe.

Do not think that it is *only* on the factory production line that accidents happen. The majority of accidents fall into the following categories.

- Lifting incorrectly — boxes of stationery can be very heavy.
- Slips and trips — spillages on linoleum or stone floors and stairs. Trips over torn carpet, shifted carpet tiles, or other obstructions.
- Trailing wires — the bane of the electronic age!

These can all happen in the office, so remember: **safety is *your* responsibility!**

9

THE BEST USE OF TIME

If there is one thing which is common to all supervisors, it is their lack of time. We all agree that if only we had more time, we could do so many things that much better. If only supervisors had the time to communicate, to brief, to train, to delegate, to discuss personal and professional problems, how much better life would be. Instead of which, many of these very important aspects are missed because there is too much work to be done; there is too little time.

But are we making best use of our time? Is it worth spending time in the short-term to make better use of time in the long-term. The answer is invariably a resounding 'Yes'.

Time analysis

Only when we analyse our time will we be able to fully evaluate where time is being wasted; where we need to re-establish our priorities. For when we review time spent in our mind's eye, the memory plays tricks on us, convincing us that items that we considered valuable and worthwhile took no time at all to complete, whereas more trivial and mundane items, items that we did not enjoy doing or did not really want to do, seemed to take forever. True statistical analysis will prove this image to be false and highly distorted. The truth will only become apparent if we discipline ourselves to run a time log, noting down how we spend each minute of the working day. Then analyse that statistical log into the various functions that your job requires. Prioritise this into order of importance and you will then get a true picture of how you spend your time.

Then ask yourself the following questions.

● Am I spending enough time on the more important matters?

- Can I reduce the time being spent on the less important matters?
- Can I delegate any jobs?
- Are all the jobs still relevant or can they be eliminated?
- Have I any time left for 'nothing in particular'?

Once you have sorted out your priorities, it is possible to work out a rough programme of day-to-day activities. Some jobs must be done daily, some weekly, some at longer intervals, and a simple system is needed to ensure that none is overlooked.

You can, for example, keep a wall calendar showing (by various markings) completion dates, appointments, special jobs, etc. Alternatively, a desk diary showing actions to be taken on particular days can be maintained. Whatever you decide, keep it simple and have, as your sole object, a desire to organise your time effectively.

10

HOW ARE YOU DOING?

In a job as complex as supervising, it is essential to step back every now and again to take a look at how you are doing. There are several possible ways to examine the record of your section over a given period in respect of:

- volume of work
- waste of time and/or materials
- absenteeism and staff turnover
- punctuality
- staff attitudes towards changes and new equipment
- team effort.

Review any grievance or complaints you have had to deal with. Are they a symptom of general dissatisfaction? Do they point to any particular faults in the section? Do they always come from the same people?

Analyse the mistakes that have occurred. Why did they go wrong? Take a look at yourself. Can you improve?

To be effective in your job you must:

- know what you are meant to be doing
- know where you fit in
- adopt efficient working methods and controls
- have the confidence and support of your team.

Above all, you must make a positive effort to understand people. The qualities most admired in a working team leader are seen to be:

- know your job and do it well
- never panic

- firm and fair, having neither favourites nor scapegoats
- decisive and consistent, so that your team knows exactly where it stands
- constant, good humoured and imaginative, so that your team really enjoys working for you.

Easy to say; more difficult to achieve!

APPENDICES

APPENDIX 1

COMPANY KNOWLEDGE

1 What is the main purpose of your company?
2 What service does it provide, and to whom?
3 What does your section contribute to this?
4 Is yours a public company? If not, what type is it?
5 What did your company's last balance sheet reveal?
6 What are the conditions of employment (holidays, overtime, etc)?
7 Has the company got a staff handbook? Have you read it recently?
8 What is the company's attitude to staff committees and joint consultation?
9 What part do unions or staff associations play in the company's affairs?
10 Who is your Health and Safety Officer? Where is the accident book kept?

APPENDIX 2

WHERE DO YOU FIT IN?

1 To whom are you immediately responsible?
2 To whom do you report in that person's absence?
3 Can you trace the line of authority from yourself to the top and bottom of the company?
4 Is the line clear?
5 How many employees are responsible to you?
6 Is it a manageable number? If not, what do you do about it?
7 Do you have regular contact with your manager?
8 What are your limits of authority?
9 Who is your deputy who acts in your absence?
10 What do your fellow supervisors do?
11 Do you meet them regularly?
12 Do you know the specialists in your company (i.e. personnel, training, accounts, etc.)?

APPENDIX 3

IS THIS YOUR JOB?

1 Determining the number of staff required in your section.
2 Selecting new staff.
3 Induction of new staff.
4 Training staff on-the-job.
5 Authorising leave of absence.
6 Arranging overtime.
7 Recommending merit awards.
8 Ensuring compliance with relevant statutory regulations.
9 Keeping various records.
10 Making staff reports.
11 Suggesting improved methods of work.
12 Keeping a check on costs and wastage.
13 Checking work.
14 Upgrading performance.
15 Keeping an eye on adequacy and effectiveness of furniture and equipment.
16 Supervising maintenance, cleaning and storage of items.
17 Keeping up-to-date with new ideas and new equipment and recommending their use where advisable.
18 Controlling flow of work through section.
19 Maintaining working team.
20 Planning for the future.
21 Making decisions about technical, organisational and human problems.

APPENDIX 4

SUBJECTS FOR TEAM BRIEFING

Some examples of subjects to be covered in a briefing session:

- output
- financial results
- targets
- quality
- safety
- fire drill
- housekeeping
- new methods
- correcting 'grapevine' rumours
- office reorganisation
- advertising
- deadlines
- customer/client service
- telephone manner
- complaints
- training
- changes in local personnel
- 'save it' campaign.